I WISH "I" COULD BE A BOY

SREEHARI .NC

" I dedicate this book to all the people who can relate to this story and also feel shy to write a book or poem, thinking about people's reactions. you can do it! Let's support each other. Enjoy the story".

Thanking all the people who supported me and special credit to my friend "zebaazmi" who inspired me to write this book.

Contents

Title

I Wish "I"could be a boy

SREEHARI.NC

Preface

About the Author ;

My life journey started In India, where I was born in 2003. I am not that of an academic person, I was totally interested in sports and extra-curricular activities. I used to be in the last bench or 2 rows front but not in the first bench. I was so much involved in tennis, and badminton. but when I reached 18, that's where I got to know that I can write a poem. I had a very good friend for me, who is traveling with me even now. by seeing her write poems, I just tried once where there were only small errors, but the poem turned out beautiful. Then I decided to write poems, quotes, and stories. The pandemic made me use time and write poems that I never thought I would write. I believe though I wrote poems or stories few were laughing, and that did make me down but not for a long time until I realized that they don't have the guts or courage to express their feelings. We try and fail, again we do that, but we never give up. so we are not called losers as many haven't taken a step to try it. you don't need to get a medal or cup to prove your victory, you can do your work silently and get your victory. only you can stop yourself, no person or words can stop you. thanking everyone who got this book. Sending you all love and positivity.

CHAPTER ONE

THE BABY, BOY!

We count people's age by week and then to months and years similarly, A boy child was born.his parents, relatives, and people around him were so happy and filled with joy . he was a color of cherry with beautiful eyes and a silent smile. later, he started to crawl and use the baby walker, going wroom from this end to that end, after a few months his parents named him NICK.

Nick was so active but a naughty kid indeed, spilling all the food, screaming at mid-nights, etc . after a few years, he was sent to kindergarten school and enrolled in PRE-KG. nick felt very anxious and started to cry when he stepped into the school on his first day . he became silent for a few days until he started to get a few friends and became used to the school environment.

He became the teacher's favorite kid as he was very obedient and got excellent grades in his pre-kg. the same thing happened in LKG as well. but when he came to UKG, that's where his notorious began

He became so frustrated and angry at the people near him who started to tease him. But he was somewhat excelling in his grades . he then participated in theatre events, sports, etc.

He hated one of his subject teachers as she started to beat him for small reasons, after all the incidents he got his final exam he got great grades and he was happy he completed kindergarten, Nick started to see a new set of people as he went to 1st grade and only a few were known to him . as he started to get interested in his extracurricular activities, his study hours or his grades started to decline a little.

Meanwhile the subject teacher he hated the most, returned, this time he thought everything would go smoothly. That was just a thought, not in reality. he became even more frustrated as the teacher started to punish him and a few other people. he got a cup and a medal for his excellence in his extra-curricular activities and not in his studies. when his 1st grade got over, he went and said to his parents about the school system and that he hated going to school.

Then, his parents moved him to an international school where he didn't cry while going to school as he was welcomed and treated humbly. nick was made to sit at 2nd grade and everything started to look new to him as his old school was congested and was not that clean.

Nick loved the environment so much as the days kept passing by. His teachers and the school staff were very friendly. he was told to talk only in English and not in his mother tongue, he found it hard in talking English as he is not used to it.

But somehow he got to know from teachers, and rectify the mistakes that he used to make. looking into the study wise he was a good student but was not scoring like his pre-kg. his parents were happy that he got into a good school, learning and talking in English.

Besides participating in events nick did not fail to score in his studies. He then got his annual exams and got good grades. Nick was promoted to grade 3, where was told to use a pen to write instead of a pencil. By scribbling and writing in crooked form, nick got used to writing in pen.

The same year nick participated in a dance for his annual day, where he was more excited to perform on stage and same as last year he got appreciation from his parents and teachers.

After his annual exams got over, during his 4th grade he was told to participate in any sport he wishes for. he chose tennis as he was going to practice for more than a year. He got certificates and appreciation as he was awarded as the winner and runner-up for a few events.

His grade started to go down as his interest started to fail in his studies and took a major interest in his extra-curricular activities and sports.

Nick, after going through lots of struggles in his academics,he was promoted to 5th grade, where things happened the same as the last year, but he became more notorious compared to the previous years and started to get scoldings and words from his parents and teachers.

but he was not bet as he got in his kindergarten.

Nick was excelling in sports, annual day, and sports day but failed to meet the expectations in his grade. nick started to feel notice a slight change in his mind and body as days passes by.

CHAPTER TWO

MEETING HIS PRE-ADULT

When nick was at the end of his 5th grade, he noticed some change in his body until when he completed his 5th grade and 6th grade in mid of 7th he noticed his center throat moving front, and the people around him started to tell him that his voice is changing a little.

Nick felt weird noticing all the change. After a few days he also noticed the same with his friends, nick started to question his friends "why is our throat coming out straight sharp?" and hair growing in your arms and leg.

Nick was still wondering what was happening between humans. Later, he found out that he met his adolescent times. he started to be different and act different.

Nick became very reactive, sensitive, and angry toward the people who started to blame or tease him. Nick hated being in art class as the teacher resembled his kindergarten teacher being rude and harsh. he got into so many troubles in 8th grade and was a menace to people.

He wasn't proper in completing his work, and assignments, and least in grades. nick went from being the first at his pre-school and being one of the least marks in the class, but still, he managed to get certificates and awards in his dance, theatre acts, and sports.

He participated in 2 more sports such as badminton and throwball. Nick was even good in these 2 sports too. now, what happens is you reach your teenage, you became a different human and majorly you fall in love with the opposite gender. the same thing happened to nick and his friends.

Nick started to talk to everyone. He didn't mind whether it was his elder of younger. He became well-known among people. He started to feel excited and happy as he was recognized everywhere in school. but that is where the problem began. When nick got into a problem, everyone started to question him about the problem, and nick felt guilty explaining it.

But besides all the problems he was the happiest soul. During the 11ᵗʰ grade, he became one of the huge and fattest people in his class because of his binge eating of fast food. In fact, nick started to have pizza and cola every day or thrice a week, His parents started to warn him about the food intake, but nick did not care. His size went all away from small to extra-large.

His friend's circle became small during his senior grade, people started to tease him and abuse him for his size. Luckily, he had a few friends who was having his back and motivated him that it is okay.

Nick did not give up, he enjoyed his lifestyle and was a happy soul, nick became the laziest person too! nick use to call his friends nearby just to pick up the water bottle and when he jumps into the swimming pool, damn the water splashed out.

In between, nick goes into depression as he was very confused about his life. he did not talk to his parents or wasn't socializing with anyone except his 1 best friend, his parents had no clue what was going on in his mind. only his 1 best friend knows what and why is in the state. he was not willing to explain to his parents why is he in that state.

After a month, his best friend then advises and tells him the reality, and he too gets a clear view of what is he going to do. He then becomes normal and starts to laugh and smile and reunite with everyone. But his parents never got the opportunity to know the reason behind his depression.

He was always there for his friends to help. He was also very attached to his teachers as he was very friendly and humorous.

During his last year of school, he had a huge love for a girl who was in another school in the same town. they got to know each other via a birthday party. They became good friends at first, but later on, after a year he expressed his love for her.

She was quite in shock but stated a few reasons, but nick gave time to her to express what she feels. In-between days she and nick spent an amazing time together. Hanging out, late-night talking, etc . quite days later she agreed to nick's proposal, by giving a tiny letter.

Nick had butterflies in his stomach on that day . she and nick were so happy being together, and where his and her friends were happy indeed by seeing them and even his friends were in a relationship too!

They had a wonderful time together. nick use to visit her house sometimes and spend time with her family and pets. he also became very close to her neighbors, but no one knows both are in a relationship, even nick's parents.

Sometimes, nick use to be extra nice to her by taking her out or visiting her house often. sometimes nick use to call his friends and introduce her to them, and so does she. they all felt very surrounded and helped each other. She was always there when nick requires help and even nick helped her with solving a lot of issues.

But later, after months things did not go as normally as it was, and both got into arguments for a few days, where the communication would be minimal until they are sorted out.

After 8-9 months, nick felt quite wrong in her actions and nick was not able to break with her as nick was very attached and emotionally touched to her. nick was pretending to be happy whenever she talks. later on, nick got a word with her friend telling him all the issues and things that happened and telling him he is unstable to tell anything now.

After a few days, nick listened to the words of his friend and he broke up with her. nick was not having a great time for a few days as the issue was revolving In his mind constantly, he was not able to focus on a few things, but did not give up hope

Suddenly there was a virus outbreak and the pandemic started, nick threw everything and started to focus on his own body, which was a typical bear. most people gained weight and were suffering from lots of physical and mental aches, during the pandemic.

He was also going through lot of pain physically and mentally. he started to get panic attacks as he was thinking too much about his size and also because he got covid aswell. it all disappeared after few weeks but all that he was undergoing was alone.

After a year and a half passed nick came to the shape that he was thinking of and successfully attained the goal, he was extremely emotional by seeing his own body from before and now. he gained a lot of confidence, his friends started to appreciate his efforts. but, few were not accepting what nick did. nick felt there will be criticism always when you do something, so he did not care what other people were telling.

When nick turned 19, he organized a birthday party with 8-10 people. he invited all for lunch. all had a great time by sharing their food, telling stories, and of course more laughter and giggles.

CHAPTER THREE

THE REALIZATION

When nick turned 19, he organized a birthday party with 8-10 people. nick had a great time with them and after days nick and his friends joined college. He and his friends were offered the course they wished for, but everyone was separate from each other as it was a different place. somehow they get to visit on holidays and spend a good time.

All were very happy going into college, nick got to see new people and he became so kind and good to people around him . he started to get love and positivity from his fellow mates. He loved his college syllabus and the way it was taught to him. His doubts were all cleared whenever he raised a question.

Though he was not a human who was always in studies like his few peers, he understood most of the things being taught. he loved things being done practically.

he got really good grades in practical but average in the theory .once he completes his first sem, he gets a short exam holiday of around 10-15 days where one day there was huge noise outside his room, nick got panicked and went out of his room to check what was happening, he noticed small issues was going in his home, nick tries to involve but he is told to stay in the room.

After all the holidays got over, nick returns to his college. 2 days after he sits in his room, and starts to cry in grief . his friend asked him, why he was crying all of a sudden and he tells :

when "I was brought up as a kid knowing nothing and if I talks about something wrong also, people wouldn't mind, relatives and people were all around to take care of me, enjoy and play with me by having the huge smile and small giggles and at last I was welcomed everywhere.

when I grew up as a teenager I was pampered not to do this and do that and made up being a self-healing machine and used everywhere just as a tiny temporary tool. Being abused by words which is the worst thing for a human and being mentally ill, just smiling fake and reacting to the people around me as if I was totally okay,

Now as an adult I should think about what I speak, I shouldn't act childish, I should not cry as I am a grown man and I should not do what I did In my childhood or early teen and now I am not welcomed by anyone except my colleagues", says nick very emotionally to his family. he also adds, you people think depression or mental illness is just for people who earn money or work, that's not true. everyone is prone to that just like the virus.

-

Does the virus affect only the poor and all riches are happy?

He also tells that family is the priority, but things happening in front of him seem like the family is nothing and not helpful. this is when he realizes, I WISH I COULD BE A BOY!

Now I read this book and think,

I WISH I COULD BE A BOY!

<u>THE END!</u>

The Actual Truth

1. Mental illness is common for everyone. so take care.

2. It is okay for a man or woman to cry, it does not make them weak .they just express their emotions. keeping it inside might harm you as well.

3. It is okay to have minimal people around you, make sure they support you and correct your mistakes.

4. You are your company, go out alone, be thankful to yourself, do what you love, and stay happy and lovely.

5. You are worth living.

6. Be kind and show gratitude.

7. Never fail to spread love and positivity.

8. Do what you love, stay happy & time is limited.

9. There are obviously mistakes everywhere, and its totally fine to make.

STAY STRONG!

Gratitude

THANKING ALL MY FRIENDS AND FAMILY MEMBERS WHO GAVE YOUR HELP AND SUPPORT! AND YES THIS STORY IS BASED ON MANY "BOYS" LIFE.

SPECIAL THANKS TO :

- **SRUTHIKA**

- **NAFFIA**

- **HARANI**

- **HARIKISHAN, for pushing me to do what I love and showing tremendous love.**

WITH A WHOLE HEART THANKING ALL THE READERS WHO TOOK THE EFFORT AND BOUGHT THIS !

DEEP CONDOLENCES TO THE PEOPLE WHO DIED DUE TO COVID!